Routes and journe

Contents

Teachers' notes	1
I come to school with	5
On the way to school I saw...	6
On the way to school I heard...	7
Journey to school	8
Rush hour traffic	9
People who help on our journeys – 1	10
People who help on our journeys – 2	11
Crossing the road	12
Going on holiday	13
Crossing the road dominoes	14 - 17
Crossing the road safely	18
Accident!	19

Going to Granny's	—
Going to the shop	21
Town and country – 1	22
Town and country – 2	23
Safety on journeys	24 - 25
People and journeys	26
Letter to Switzerland	27
Routes from Ben's home	28
Tracks and routes	29
Journeys – 1	30
Journeys – 2	31
The crash	32

Teachers' notes

The activities in this book aim to support the implementation of the National Curriculum for geography at Levels 1 to 3. The activities are not designed to be teaching tools in their own right, but rather to offer children the opportunity to practise geographical skills and knowledge they have acquired.

It is important to explain the purpose of each activity at the start, in order to focus the children's energy on that aspect of the task and to prevent the sheets being perceived as mere 'colouring activities'.

Aims of this book

● To highlight the many different journeys and routes children make on a regular basis.
● To help children think about the detail of those routes and journeys, in particular the main 'landmarks' along those routes.
● To demonstrate that the 'landmarks' people see on their journeys vary depending on whether they live in a town or in the country.
● To help children visualise journeys and routes as a sequence, with a start, a middle and an end.
● To encourage children to develop ideas about personal safety in relation to all journeys they make, but particularly in relation to their daily journeys to and from school.
● To encourage children to think about other types of journeys and routes, such as the journey of a letter.

Reproducing the activities

Most teachers will want to photocopy the activities on to white paper but with certain activities they may also consider copying on to coloured paper or card. This is particularly the

case with pages 14 to 17 (Dominoes) and 24 to 25 (Snakes and ladders) where copying on to card and covering with clear self-adhesive plastic film will ensure that the materials have a much longer life.

Geographical background

Journeys and routes are a very important part of young children's geographical development. Journeys are the ways in which children explore their local environment and develop ideas about the buildings, people, roads and other features which make up that environment. Such journeys also allow children to develop basic geographical ideas about routes in relation to maps and to begin to think critically about the local environment.

It is important to encourage children to think carefully about things they see on a regular basis in their local environment. Often, it seems that children walk or travel through the local environment with their eyes shut! It is vital to their geographical development for them to think about the landmarks, people and places in that environment, identifying the locations of those different places and people as well as considering their characteristics.

Taking children on short journeys around the school will encourage them to think about how to plan a route (for example, from their classroom to the hall), and to consider the things they will pass on the way. Providing guidance to a new member of the class (real or imaginary) on how to get to important places around the school, such as the hall or the secretary's office, can provide another stimulus for investigating routes and journeys. A short walk around the

school grounds and into the immediate environment can be the next step in developing children's ideas about longer routes and journeys. In this way, a concentric approach can be adopted to the topic, in which children gradually investigate longer and more complex journeys as they grow and develop.

Other members of the family can also be involved in the learning process. The role of adults in helping children deal with ideas about personal safety is important, in addition to considerations about the different journeys made by different members of the family.

Notes on individual activities

Page 5: I come to school with ...

Aim: to encourage children to think about the people who form part of their environment. Immediate family members are the first to form part of this environment and the aim is to link this to the journeys children make.

Preparation and practice: the children are asked to draw themselves and a friend but they could go on to draw their own sheets for other friends. The person they come to school with should be an adult, so before starting the activity get the children to talk about which adults accompany them and why it is important to have help from adults over things such as crossing busy roads.

Extension: draw other adults seen on the way to school or on other journeys.

Pages 6 and 7: On the way to school I saw/ On the way to school I heard

Aim: to make children think carefully about things they see and hear on one particular route. This is also a sorting exercise.

Preparation and practice: the children will need a large sheet of blank paper on which to stick the pictures of the things they see, and hear, on the way to school. Use different coloured paper for things seen and for things heard. Point out that they should *not* cut out and stick in things they do not see or hear on their journey. Ask them to draw their own pictures of things they see, and hear, which are not shown on the sheets.

Extension: draw, colour and sort things you see or hear on other journeys, for example to the shops.

Page 8: Journey to school

Aim: to help children realise that journeys consist of a series of stages, and that one stage cannot start before the previous one has finished. Sequencing is a basic activity for understanding routes and journeys.

Preparation and practice: discuss what each picture shows before the children start colouring

them in and selecting the correct sentences. They will need a large sheet of sugar paper on which to stick the sorted pictures. Can they draw and sequence pictures of their own journeys to school?

Extension: draw and sequence pictures of other journeys, such as to visit a relative or friend.

Page 9: Rush hour traffic

Aim: to encourage children to imagine what different people would say about a common feature of most journeys, in this case rush hour traffic jams.

Preparation and practice: discuss with the children what is going on in the picture and what people might be saying.

Extension: draw pictures of other common scenes connected with journeys, such as a visit to a bus or train station, waiting in an airport lounge and so on.

Pages 10 and 11: People who help on our journeys – 1 and 2

Aim: to focus children's thinking on people to whom they can turn for help on journeys and along routes. This is also a shape activity.

Preparation and practice: these are two cut, match and stick activities in which the figures at the top of the page should help the children arrange the different shapes in the correct order. Ask them to name the various shapes.

Extension: make other figures of people who help on journeys from similar shapes, for example a parent or bus driver.

Page 12: Crossing the road

Aim: to encourage children to think about personal safety in the environment. This is an important sequencing activity.

Preparation and practice: discuss with the children the correct way to cross a busy road. Ask them to talk about do's and don'ts. Discuss what is shown in each picture. Can the children arrange the completed pictures in a straight line sequence?

Extension: practise correct procedures for crossing busy roads in the hall or playground.

Page 13: Going on holiday

Aim: to encourage children to think about other journeys they make which are not as frequent as those to school or to the shops.

Preparation and practice: the sentences provide a simple outline for a story based on preparing for a holiday journey. Children can add their own sentences to continue the story on the back of the sheet.

Extension: write sentences for other, less frequent journeys, such as to the dentist or optician.

Pages 14, 15, 16 and 17: Crossing the road dominoes

Aim: to encourage road safety awareness.
Preparation and practice: copy the sheets on to stiff paper or card. Talk to the children about different ways of crossing roads. Make sure they understand the meaning of all the words involved. The game can then be played with groups of four children, each with one set of the dominoes. The winner is the first person to match up all their dominoes.
Extension: practise correct procedures for crossing busy roads in the hall or playground.

Page 18: Crossing the road safely

Aim: to encourage road safety awareness.
Preparation and practice: discuss what is shown in each picture and why it is a safe way of crossing a busy road. Use the pictures and labels for games of snap.
Extension: draw pictures and write the names of other features in the environment which help to cross busy roads safely, for example a crossing warden, railings beside a road directing children to a crossing.

Page 19: Accident!

Aim: to help children focus on what is safe and what is unsafe behaviour in the environment, linking the features of the environment to human activity.
Preparation and practice: ask the children to describe what is happening in each picture and look at why the accident has taken place. After they have sequenced the pictures the children can continue the story of the child's recovery in hospital and journey home with parents.
Extension: draw and sequence pictures of a different kind of accident, for instance what might happen to children playing a game of football near a busy road.

Pages 20 and 21: Going to Granny's/ Going to the shop

Aim: to encourage children to think about how routes change direction. Use right and left as ways of describing direction.
Preparation and practice: Going to Granny's – after drawing a route through the maze children can draw their own mazes. Going to the shop – revise left and right with the children before starting this activity. Make sure they understand on which parts of the picture they have to put the crosses and circles, i.e. where they change direction.
Extension: draw other mazes for routes, such as from school to the sweet shop or from home to the swimming baths.

Pages 22 and 23: Town and country – 1 and 2

Aim: to encourage children to think about how the same journey (i.e. from home to school) can be very different in different parts of the UK. The main contrast is between urban and rural scenes.
Preparation and practice: the illustrations from Town and country – 1 need to be matched with the correct section on the Venn diagram. You will need to explain that some objects can be found in both town and country and so need to go in the section where the sets overlap. Children can draw other objects to add to the diagram.
Extension: draw sets of things children hear on town or country journeys.

Pages 24 and 25: Safety on journeys

Aim: to focus on some of the dangers children face on journeys and how those dangers may be avoided.
Preparation and practice: the children will need coloured counters and a die to play the game. Copy the board on to an A3 sheet and make sure that children understand that they go up ladders and down snakes. Discuss how each picture shows either an element of safety or an element of danger.
Extension: add other pictures to the game to show elements of both danger and safety, such as running into the road after a ball or crossing safely with a crossing warden.

Page 26: People and journeys

Aim: to encourage children to look more carefully at people in uniform whom they see on their journeys. This will also link journeys with types of transport.
Preparation and practice: discuss with the children what vehicles and persons are shown in each picture before starting the activity. Talk about the job each person does and how it is related to journeys. Match the people with the vehicles.
Extension: talk about the job each person does and why it is important.

Page 27: Letter to Switzerland

Aim: to encourage children to think about different types of journeys, such as those made by parcels or letters.
Preparation and practice: talk to the children about sending letters to people in their own country and abroad. Discuss the contents of addresses and why these are so important. Make sure that the children know what each picture shows, and what homes in Switzerland look like.
Extension: draw and sequence pictures of other journeys, for example milk from farm to shop or doorstep.

Page 28: Routes from Ben's home

Aim: to begin the development of basic mapwork skills by focusing on key landmarks shown on a picture map.

Preparation and practice: make sure the children know where Ben lives and that the routes they draw must follow the roads. Talk about the things Ben will see on his journey, and the order in which he will see them.

Extension: draw a picture map of things passed on the way from school to home.

Page 29: Tracks and routes

Aim: to extend the idea of journeys from those made by people, to those made by animals.

Preparation and practice: talk to the children about the different tracks made by people, birds and animals and how these show up in snow or mud.

Extension: draw footprints of a bear or a dog to make a journey.

Pages 30 and 31: Journeys – 1 and 2

Aim: to encourage children to think carefully about the key landmark features in their environment and how these are important in journeys.

Preparation and practice: talk to the children about Journeys – 1 and show how the pictures relate to the words used in the boxes. Explain that the words in the boxes give an excellent summary of the journey, showing the places John passed and the order in which he passed them. Ask the children to use the four journeys on activity sheet 2 to summarise some of their own important journeys, for example from home to visit relatives or from home to school. Some children may prefer to draw pictures of landmarks they pass on their journey before they fill in the names of these landmarks on the sheet.

Extension: draw pictures of typical landmark features, such as shops, post office, garage, pub, road junction, park and so on.

Page 32: The crash

Aim: to encourage children to imagine journeys they or other people may make, taking into account what might happen and what the environment might be like.

Preparation and practice: this activity gives children the security of writing a story based on pictures. Discuss with them what each picture shows and how the story of the journey might end. In particular talk about what pictures might be in each box and how this will affect what they write.

Extension: draw a picture story of other journeys for friends to complete.

National Curriculum: Geography

The activities in this book support the following requirements of the PoS for KS1 from the geography National Curriculum:

Geographical skills
Pupils should be taught to develop and use the following geographical skills:
● observe, question and record, and communicate ideas and information;
● make maps and plans of real and imaginary places, using pictures and symbols;
● use globes, maps and plans at a variety of scales;
● use secondary sources to obtain geographical information.

Places
Pupils should be taught:
● about the main physical and human features that give the localities their character;
● about the effects of weather on people and their surroundings;
● how land and buildings are used;

Themes
Pupils should be taught:
● to express views on the attractive and unattractive features of the environment concerned.

Scottish 5 - 14 Curriculum: Environmental studies – Social subjects

Attainment outcome	Strand	Target	Level
Understanding people and places	Knowledge and understanding	Aspects of the physical and built environment. Ways in which places have affected people and people have used and affected places.	A
	Recording and presenting	Record collected evidence by drawing pictures, making models and writing captions and short pieces.	A

I come to school with...

● Draw a picture of yourself in the first box.

● Now draw a picture of a grown-up you come
to school with in the box below.

● Draw a friend in the second box.

● Draw a picture of a grown-up they come to school with.

On the way to school I saw...

● Colour in and cut out the things you see on your way to school.

● Stick them on to a large piece of paper.

 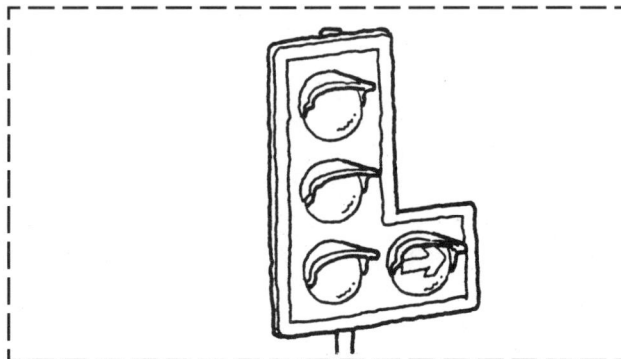

On the way to school I heard...

● Colour in and cut out all the things you heard on your way to school.

● Stick them on to a large piece of paper.

Journey to school

The pictures show a journey to school.

● Choose the correct sentence from the list below
to write under each picture.

Getting off the bus	**Waiting for the bus**
Getting on the bus	**Crossing the road to school**

● Colour in the pictures then cut them out and put them in order.

Rush hour traffic

The picture shows the rush hour in town.

● Look at the picture. What is everyone saying?
Write their words in the speech bubbles.

People who help on our journeys – 1

● Colour in the shapes below and then cut them out.

● Now can you stick them together to make a person who helps us cross the road?

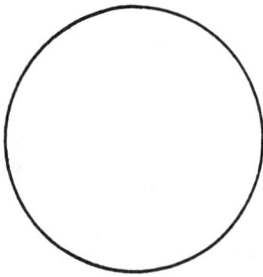

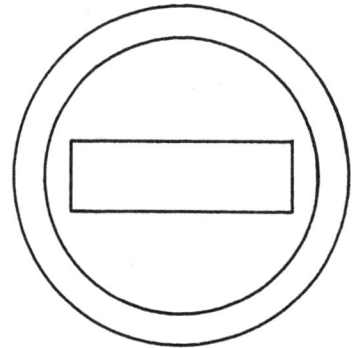

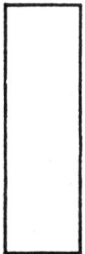

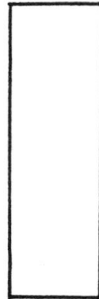

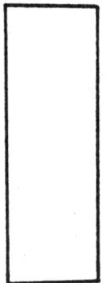

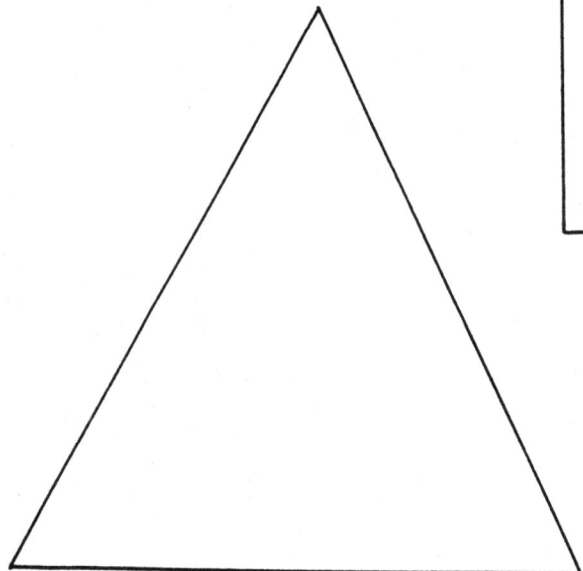

People who help on our journeys – 2

● Colour in the shapes below and then cut them out.

● Now can you stick them together to make a policeman?

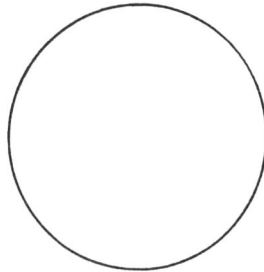

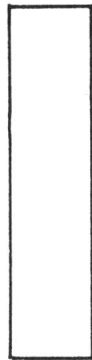

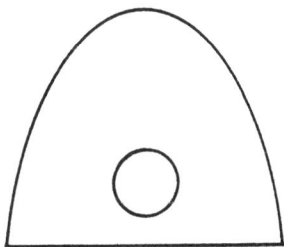

Crossing the road

● The pictures below show how to cross the road but are they in the correct order?

● Colour them in.

● Now cut them out and arrange them in the correct order.

Going on holiday

● Look at the sentences below and sentence endings beside the picture. Can you match them together to make a story? Write the endings in the correct spaces.

On the day we went on holiday _____

I dressed _____

I could not find _____

I looked _____

I thought _____

Then dad said _____

Sure enough, _____

in a hurry.

I woke up early.

'Look under the bed.'

my camera.

'I have lost it.'

in the cupboard.

there was my camera.

Crossing the road dominoes – 1

● Cut out the cards on pages 14, 15, 16 and 17 to use as dominoes.

	foot bridge
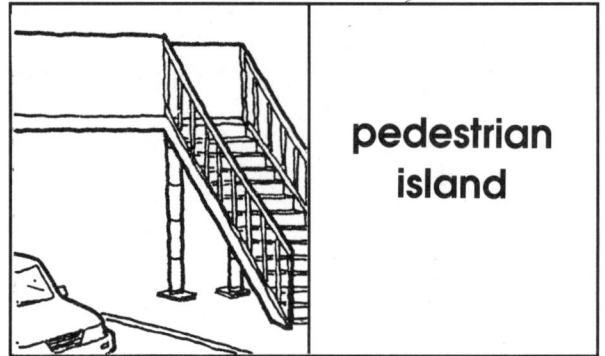	pedestrian island

traffic lights	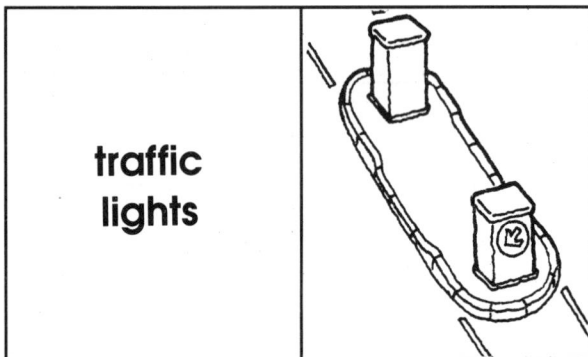
subway	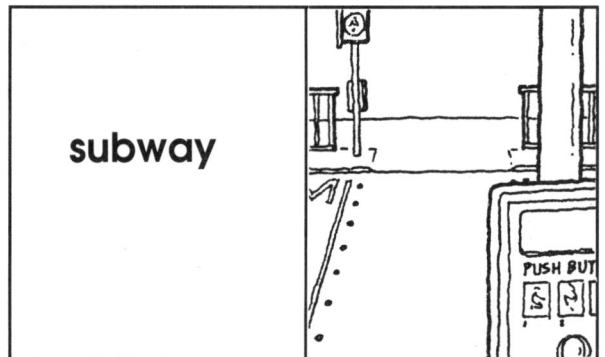

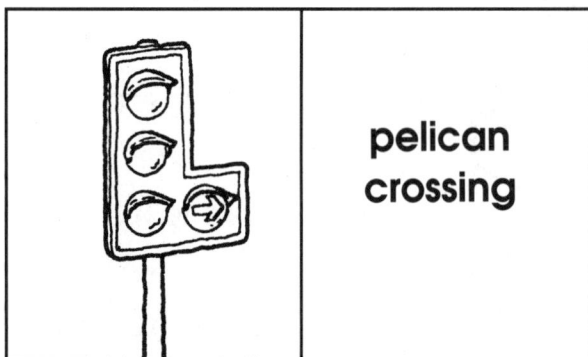	pelican crossing
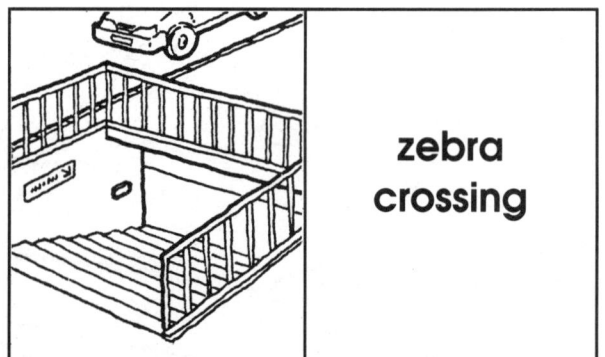	zebra crossing

Crossing the road dominoes – 2

	**foot bridge**

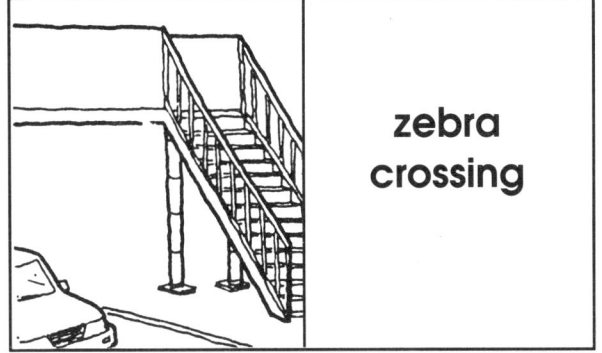	**zebra crossing**

subway	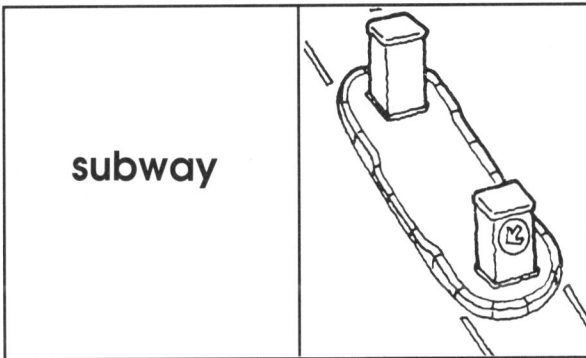

pedestrian island	

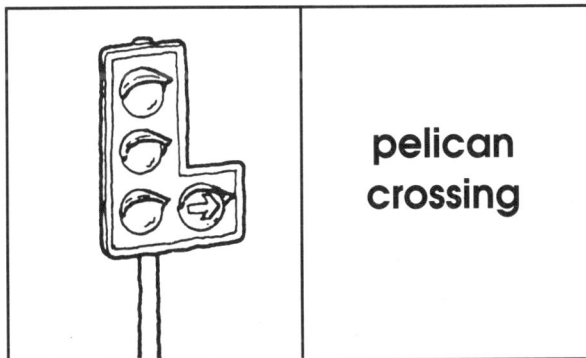	**pelican crossing**

	**traffic lights**

Crossing the road dominoes – 3

	**traffic lights**

	**pedestrian island**

pelican crossing	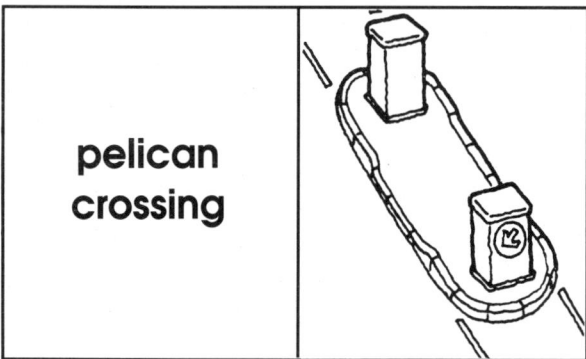

subway	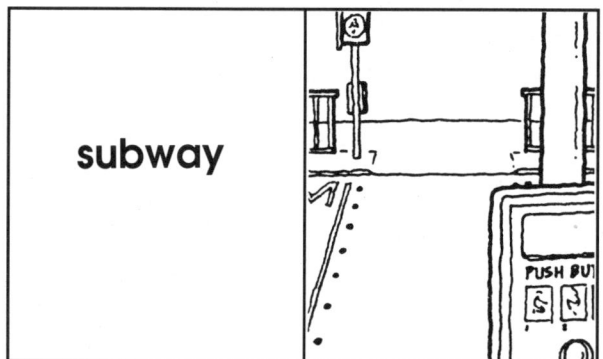

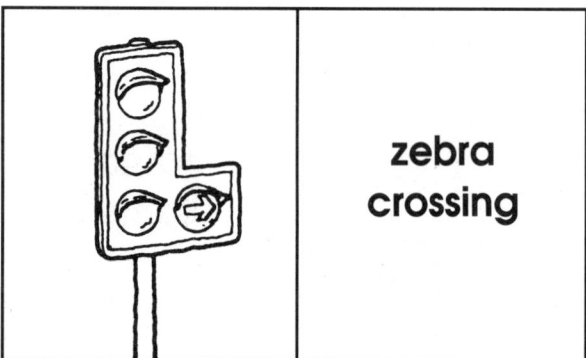	**zebra crossing**

	**foot bridge**

Crossing the road dominoes – 4

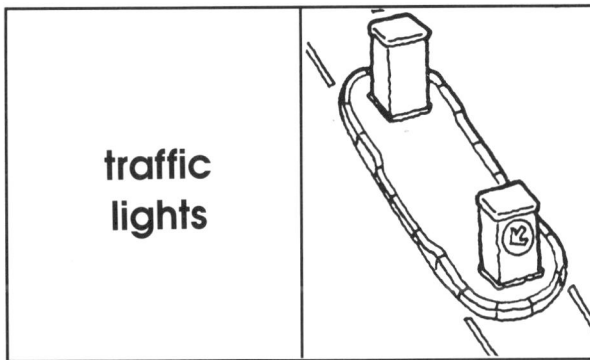

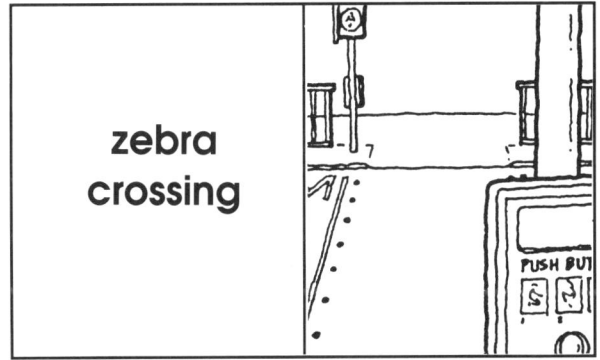

	subway

	pelican crossing

traffic lights	

zebra crossing	

	pedestrian island

PUSH BUT

	foot bridge

Crossing the road safely

The pictures show different ways of crossing the road.

● Can you match the pictures with the labels?

| pelican crossing |
| foot bridge |
| pedestrian island |
| zebra crossing |
| subway |

Accident!

The pictures show the story of a child who has an accident.

● Colour in the pictures.

● Now cut them out and put them in order to make a story.

Going to Granny's

● Help Linda find her way to Granny's house.
Which route will she need to take?

Linda

Granny

Going to the shop

- Follow the path from Sophie's home to the shop.

- Put 'O' at every right turn.

- Put 'X' at every left turn.

Town and country – 1

Jason lives in a town. Sam lives in the country.

● Look at the pictures. Which do you think are usually seen by Jason and which by Sam? Write your answers in the diagram on Town and country – 2.

Name _____

Town and country – 2

● Use this sheet with Town and country – 1.

> Write in all the things I see on my way to school.

> Write in all the things I see on my way to school.

● Name _____

Safety on journeys – 1

Finish

30	19	18
29	20	17
28	21	16
27	22	15
26	23	14
25	24	13

● Name _____

Safety on journeys – 2

7	6
8	5
9	4
10	3
11	2
12	1
	start

People and journeys

● Colour in the pictures.

● Now cut them out and put them into pairs.

Letter to Switzerland

Ruth lives in London. She is sending a birthday present to her aunt in Switzerland.

● Colour in the pictures.

● Now cut them out and arrange them in order.

Routes from Ben's home

This is a map of the area in which Ben lives.

● Draw a red line to show Ben's shortest route to school.

● Draw a green line to show Ben's longest route
from school to home.

● On the back of this sheet make a list of all the things
Ben passes on the 'red' route.

● On the back of this sheet make another list of things
Ben passes on the 'green' route.

Home

Tracks and routes

● Look at the key and draw in the tracks of the bird, the frog and Mr Riley.

● Now complete the sentences below.

NEWSAGENT

◌◌◌	Mr. Riley
◌◌	Lucy
ఒ ఒ	Frog
⅄ ⅄	Bird

Mr Riley went to _____

Lucy went to _____

The bird went to _____

The frog went to _____

Journeys – 1

This is John's journey to the Post Office:

home	
garage	
shop	
woods	
post office	

Journeys – 2

● Use this sheet to record your journeys.

From _____

To _____

_____

_____

_____

_____

From _____

To _____

_____

_____

_____

_____

From _____

To _____

_____

_____

_____

_____

From _____

To _____

_____

_____

_____

_____

Name _____

The crash

● Look at the pictures below. Can you draw pictures in the empty boxes to complete the story?

● Now can you write the story in words?